Exploring Science

The Exploring Science series is designed to familiarize young students with science topics taught in grades 4–9. The topics in each book are divided into knowledge and understanding sections, followed by exploration by means of simple projects or experiments. The topics are also sequenced from easiest to more complex, and should be worked through until the correct level of attainment for the age and ability of the student is reached. Carefully planned Test Yourself questions at the end of each topic allow the student to gain a sense of achievement on mastering the subject.

EXPLORING
SOUND

Ed Catherall

STECK-VAUGHN
LIBRARY
Austin, Texas

Exploring Science

Electricity
Magnets
Light
Soil
Sound
Weather

13231162

Cover illustrations:
Above left *A radio-wave transmitter. This is how the waves would look if they were visible.*
Above right *A megaphone used by a guide in Kyoto, Japan.*
Below *The pop singer, Michael Jackson, on tour.*

Frontispiece *The pop singer, Tina Turner.*

Editor: Elizabeth Spiers
Editor: American Editor: Susan Wilson
Series designer: Ross George

Published in the United States in 1990 by Steck–Vaughn Co., Austin, Texas, a subsidiary of National Education Corporation.

First published in 1989 by
Wayland (Publishers) Ltd

©Copyright 1989 Wayland (Publishers) Ltd

Library of Congress Cataloging-in-Publication Data

Catherall, Ed.
  Exploring sound / Ed Catherall.
    p.   cm. — (Exploring science)
  Includes bibliographical references.
  Summary: Explores the many aspects of sound, including how it travels, is received by the human ear, and can be recorded, and provides simple projects and experiments.
  ISBN 0-8114-2592-4
1. Sound—Juvenile literature.   2. Sound-waves—Experiments-Juvenile literature.   [1. Sound—Experiments. 2. Experiments.]
I. Title.   II. Series. Catherall, Ed. Exploring science.
QC225.5.C38   1989   89-38614
536—dc20   CIP AC

Typeset by Multifacit Graphics, Keyport, NJ
Printed in Italy by G. Canale C.S.p.A., Turin
Bound in the United States by Lake Book Manufacturing, Inc., Melrose Park, IL
1 2 3 4 5 6 7 8 9 0 CG 94 93 92 91 90

Contents

SOUNDS ALL AROUND

Noisy traffic and road construction—some of the many sounds all around us.

We hear sounds everywhere. Sounds help us tell what is happening around us. There are sounds inside and outside our bodies. Your body makes many sounds—for example, chewing, swallowing, breathing and stomach rumbling. Your skin makes a sound when rubbed and sometimes your joints click. Next time you go to the doctor, ask if you can listen to your heart-beat with the stethoscope.

Perhaps the most important sounds that you can make are with your voice. Sound is one of the main ways of communicating with another person. Each of us has learned a language, which means we have made sounds into words to convey our thoughts, ideas, and feelings to other peo-

ple. Many animals have their own sets of sounds for communication—for example dogs howl, bark, grown, and whimper.

Humans have many ways of producing sounds in the environment. We can play cassette tapes, switch on the television, play musical instruments, or show a movie. We can communicate over long distances using a telephone or radio. We drive noisy cars, trucks, and trains. Almost any movement in the environment makes sound—wind in the trees, water in a stream, rain on the ground, and lightning in the air. It is a noisy world.

ACTIVITIES

LISTENING TO SOUNDS OUTSIDE

1 Go outside and count how many sounds you can hear.
2 Identify what made each sound.
3 How many sounds were caused by humans?

4 Are machine noises made by humans? Explain your answer.
5 Go to different parts of your school grounds or a park. How are the sounds different? Why?

LISTENING TO SOUNDS INSIDE YOURSELF

1 Listen to yourself breathing through your nose and mouth. How are these two sounds different?
2 Cover your ears. Can you hear your heartbeat or your pulse?

3 Chew an apple, a carrot, and a piece of cheese. Describe each sound. Why are they different?
4 What other sounds can you hear from your body throughout the day?

This girl is using a stethoscope to listen to sounds inside the doctor's body. The stethoscope makes sounds louder and directs them into the listener's ears.

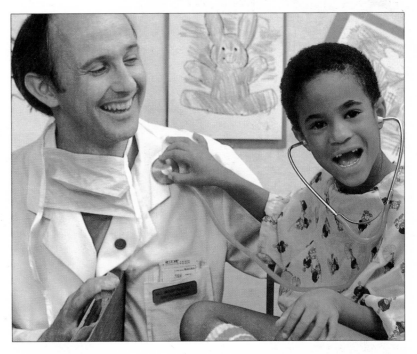

TEST YOURSELF

1. List five ways that you can make a sound.
2. Describe the sounds made by three different things in the environment.
3. List three words that describe sounds made by animals.

STUDYING SOUND

When you are listening carefully to a sound, there are three things to think about. What made the sound (the sound source)? How did the sound travel (its pathway)? What received the sound?

Sound is always made by something moving. Anything, whether it is a solid, liquid, or gas, can create sound. The energy from the moving thing is used to make the sound waves that our ears pick up.

Once a sound wave has been created, it will be transmitted (travel), as will anything that has energy. Sound waves travel through anything—any solid, liquid, or gas. However, sound will not travel through a vacuum, such as in space. A vacuum is nothing, so there is nothing there for the sound to make waves in.

Some sounds that cannot be heard by humans can be heard by other animals such as dogs. They hear a different sound range and have more sensitive ears. Sound reception includes all the devices that are sensitive to sound waves, such as telephone receivers and microphones.

Once sound waves have been received, the brain compares the new sound with a huge memory of sounds that have been heard since birth. Usually the sound is in the memory and is recognized as, for example, a motorbike or a violin.

Above *Mother and daughter in conversation. The sound source is the mother, the pathway of the sound waves is through the air, and the daughter is the receiver.*

Right *This famous poster is scientifically correct! No one can hear screaming in space, because space is a vacuum. There are no particles to conduct the sound waves.*

A L I E N

In space no one can hear you scream.

ACTIVITY

HOW GOOD IS YOUR SOUND MEMORY?

YOU NEED

- **folded paper towel**
- **a variety of small objects**
- **different coins**

✓ = correct ✗ = wrong	me	Charlie
pen		
clip	✗	✓
stone	✓	✓
rubber	✗	✗
wood	✗	✓
	✗	✗

1 Work with a friend.
2 Cover your eyes.

3 Ask your friend to drop one object at a time on a table.
4 Try to identify each object.
5 Can you name each object from the sound it makes?
6 If you get one wrong, ask your friend to tell you what it was.

7 Try the activity five times.
8 Do you get better with practice?
9 Repeat the activity with coins.
10 Can you name each coin from the sound it makes?
11 Do you get better with practice?
12 Try dropping two different coins instead of one.
13 Is it possible to identify both coins? Repeat this experiment with your friend's eyes covered, using different objects and coins.
14 Whose sound memory is better?

TEST YOURSELF

1. What makes sound waves?
2. What cannot transmit sound?
3. Why do dogs hear some sounds that humans do not hear?

SPEAKING AND SINGING

Humans use their voices for speaking, laughing, crying, and singing. How are these sounds made?

At the top of your windpipe is the larynx, which is like a hollow box. It makes a bump in the neck called the "Adam's Apple", or voice box. Inside the larynx are bands that vibrate when you speak or sing—they are called the vocal cords. One end of each cord is attached to the front wall of your larynx. The other end is attached to one of two cartilages. These cartilages can move, bringing your vocal cords together or pulling them apart.

When you breathe in, your vocal cords are pulled apart and air can pass between them. The air flows down into your lungs. When you breathe out, the vocal cords stay apart. When you speak or sing, the two cartilages move, bringing the vocal cords close together, partly blocking your air passage. The air that you breathe out is forced between the vocal cords, making them vibrate. This makes a sound. With practice, you can control your vocal cords to make a range of sounds and notes.

The vocal cords of boys and girls are roughly the same length. When a girl becomes a woman, her voice does not change much. When a boy becomes a man, his vocal cords grow longer, the larynx gets larger and his voice becomes lower.

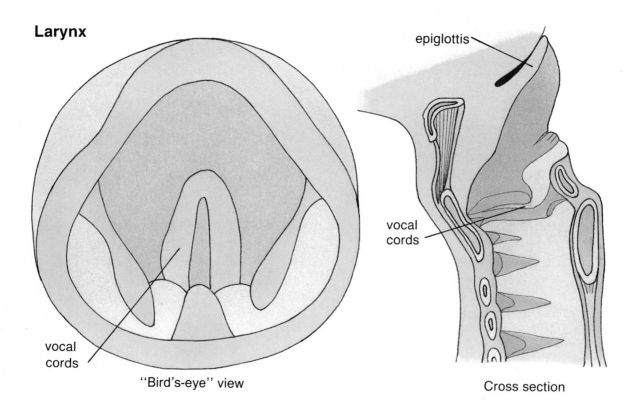

Larynx

epiglottis

vocal cords

vocal cords

"Bird's-eye" view

Cross section

ACTIVITIES

FEELING YOUR VOICE

1 Touch your throat and find the lump that is your voice box, or larynx.

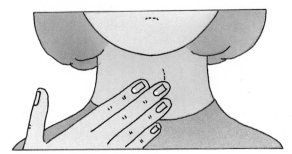

2 What can you feel when you speak?
3 Sing a low note. What can you feel?
4 Sing a high note. What can you feel?
5 Sing the same note soft, then loud. Do the two sounds feel different?
6 Sing your favorite song while holding your throat. What do you notice about your breathing and the movement of your tongue as you sing?
7 Can you sing while breathing in?
8 Say all the letters of the alphabet.
9 Notice how your tongue moves and how your vocal cords vibrate.

LANGUAGE AND WORDS

1 Which language do you speak?
2 What words do you know in a different language?
3 Listen to tapes of other languages. What differences in sound do you notice between your language and others you have heard?

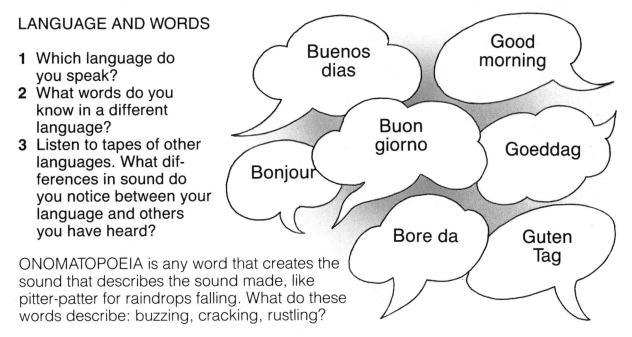

Buenos dias

Good morning

Buon giorno

Goeddag

Bonjour

Bore da

Guten Tag

ONOMATOPOEIA is any word that creates the sound that describes the sound made, like pitter-patter for raindrops falling. What do these words describe: buzzing, cracking, rustling?

TEST YOURSELF

1. Why do men's voices sound lower than women's voices?
2. How do you produce sounds when you sing?
3. Which words describe
   • a door bell's sound?
   • the sound made when a stone hits water?
   • the sound made by a falling tree?

SOUND WAVES

If you throw a stone into a calm pond, the surface of the water moves in waves or ripples. The waves spread out from the spot where the stone fell. Some of the energy of the waves is transmitted to the air above the pond and sound waves travel to your ears. Your brain interprets the sound as a splash. Someone swimming underwater can also hear the sound of the splash as the waves travel through the water. If a larger stone is thrown into the water, the disturbance is greater, the waves are larger, and the sound of the splash is louder.

When you look at the ripples moving out from the stone, you can see how high each

Sound waves moving out from a source are similar to the ripples spreading out from the point where a raindrop hits the pond.

wave is and also how close each wave is to the next one. The distance between two waves is called the wavelength. The height of each wave is called the amplitude. You can also measure the speed of the wave as it travels through the water. This is called the frequency, and is measured by counting the number of waves that pass a particular point in one second. In sound measurement, this is the number of vibrations (waves) per second.

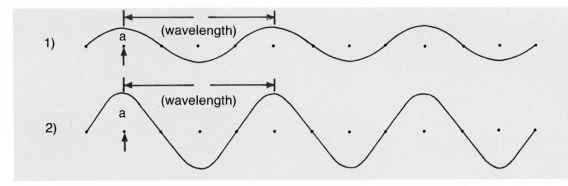

1)

2)

Above *A diagram of two waves with the same wavelength (l), but different amplitude (a). 2 is a louder sound than 1 because it has a larger amplitude.*

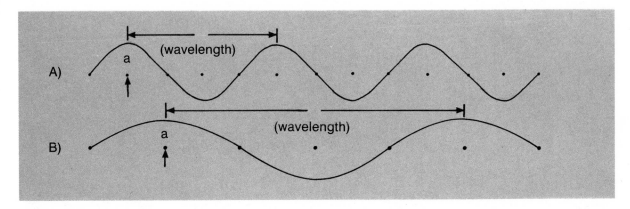

A)

B)

Above *A diagram of two waves with the same amplitude (a), but different wavelength (l). A is a higher sound than B, because it has a shorter wavelength.*

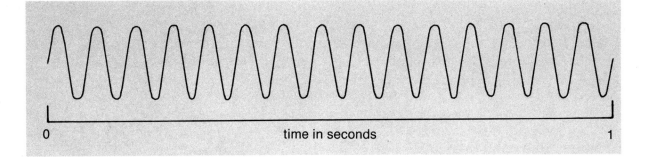

0   time in seconds   1

There are 15 waves or vibrations per second in the diagram. This is the lowest sound that a healthy, young human ear can hear. Most sounds that we hear have more vibrations per second. This means that the waves are closer together, or more frequent, so we call this a higher frequency.

This gives a higher sound. Humans can hear from about 15 to 20,000 vibrations per second. The most sensitive range of humans is from 400 to 4,000 vibrations per second. The hearing range depends on age. Older people have a shorter range of sounds that they can hear.

ACTIVITY

MAKING WATER WAVES

> ### YOU NEED
>
> - **a large glass, or clear plastic, bowl or circular tank**
> - **an eye dropper**
> - **an overhead projector and screen**

1 Half fill the bowl with water.
2 Wait for the surface to be calm.
3 Tap the water's surface at regular intervals. Watch the waves spread.

4 Tap the surface of the water harder. What happens to the waves?
5 Tap rapidly. What happens?

6 Now place the bowl on top of the overhead projector. Be careful not to spill any.
7 Wait for the water to settle down.
8 Drop water into the middle of the bowl, using the dropper.

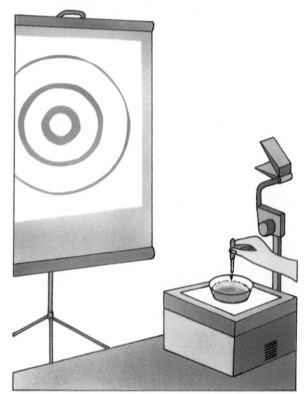

9 On the screen, watch the waves form as the drop hits the water.
10 Draw what you see.
11 Change the speed of the drops, then the height of the dropper.
12 Draw what you see in each case.

TEST YOURSELF

1. Draw a series of waves. Mark the frequency and wavelength.
2. Over what range can the human ear detect sound?
3. Do waves of higher frequency give a higher or lower sound?

SOUND WAVES IN AIR

Air is a transparent gas. Unlike water, waves created in air cannot be seen. We are aware of the waves because we can hear. Air is springy. You can feel the springiness of air when you squeeze an air-filled balloon. If you hold the balloon near your ear, you can hear sounds when you tap it with your finger. This tapping creates sound waves. It also presses on the balloon and changes the pressure slightly inside the balloon by squeezing the air particles closer together. Each tap makes a wave of high pressure—just as each tap on the surface of water creates a high wave (see page 14). The waves of high pressure in the air are the same as the high waves in the water.

The number of high-pressure waves per second gives the frequency of the note. The more waves, the higher the note.

Above *The shock/sound wave from a 3000-volt electric spark moving toward a man's face. Notice the "ripples" of sound.*

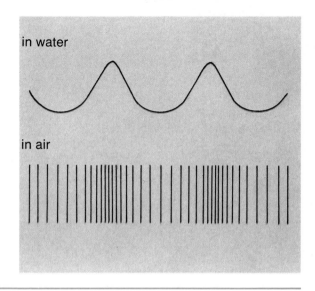

in water

in air

ACTIVITIES

MAKING WAVES

YOU NEED

- **a long jump rope**

1 Ask a friend to hold one end of the jump rope while you hold the other end. Pull the rope fairly tight.

2 Make a wave in the rope by shaking your hand.

3 Watch the wave travel down the rope toward your friend. Make several waves in the rope.
4 Make small waves close together and larger waves farther apart. How did you do this?

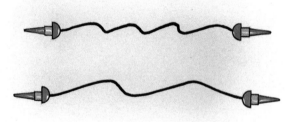

SPRING

YOU NEED

- **a hammer**
- **a nail**
- **a block of wood (not balsa wood)**
- **an old spring**
- **thread**
- **a plastic bag and some stones**

WARNING: be very careful when using a hammer.

1 Hammer the nail into the wood.
2 Hang the spring from the nail.
3 Hold the wood so that the spring hangs down.

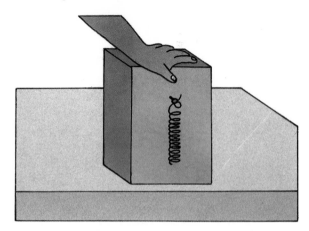

4 Tie the plastic bag to the other end of the spring, using the thread. Put stones in the bag.

5 Do not overstretch the spring.

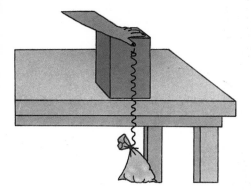

6 Pull the bag down slowly and gently, then let it go.

7 Watch the pressure wave from the bouncing bag travel up the spring.

SLINKY™ TOY

YOU NEED

- **a Slinky™ toy spring**

1 Work with a friend. Lay the Slinky™ on the floor, stretching it between you.

2 Using a quick motion, push your end of the Slinky™ toward your friend.

push

3 Watch the wave of tight coils travel down the Slinky™. This also happens when sound waves are made in air.

TEST YOURSELF

1. How is a sound wave made in air?
2. Explain what you could do to feel the springiness in air.
3. Draw a picture to show sound waves in air.

SOUND AND LENGTH

This rock musician produces sounds from his electric guitar by plucking the strings and altering their length with his fingers. The sound waves are converted to electrical energy, passed through an amplifier to make the sound louder, or for special effects, then out through the loudspeaker as sound waves again.

If you pluck a guitar string, it is disturbed, and a wave forms in the string. This wave travels in both directions until it reaches the fixed ends of the string. The wave then bounces back, causing the string to vibrate.

The vibrating string disturbs the air. This causes sound waves to travel through the air to reach your ears, and you hear the note the guitar string made. If the string is not plucked again the waves gradually get smaller and smaller and the note gets softer and softer until you can't hear it. You can make a loud note by plucking the string hard, or a soft note by plucking gently.

You can shorten the guitar string by moving your finger along the finger board. If this shorter string is plucked, the waves have a shorter wavelength. The shorter wavelength means that there are more vibrations per second (the note is at a higher pitch) than the longer wavelength (lower

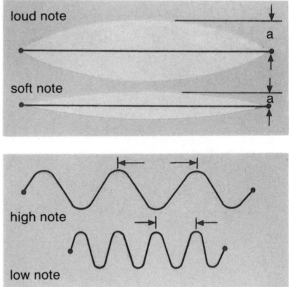

pitch). By changing the length of the string, you can create different vibrations per second and thus different notes.

ACTIVITIES

MAKING A GLOCKENSPIEL

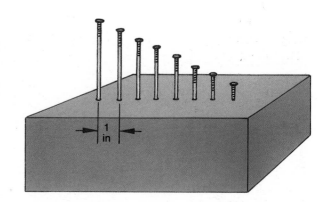

YOU NEED

- **8 large nails**
- **a pencil**
- **a thick block of wood (not balsa wood) about 10 ins. long**
- **a hammer**

WARNING: be very careful when hammering.

1 Hammer each nail into the block of wood so that it sticks up a little farther than the one before it.

2 Make sure that the nails are about an inch apart and do not touch.
3 Tap each nail with a pencil. Which nail makes the highest note? Which makes the lowest note?

TWANGING RULERS

YOU NEED

- **a wooden ruler**

1 Place the ruler on a table so that part of it sticks out over the edge.

2 Twang the ruler gently. Listen to the sound.
3 Move the ruler farther onto the table. Twang it again. How is the note different?

4 Move the ruler so that almost all of it sticks out over the edge of the table. Twang it again. How is the note different now?

TEST YOURSELF

1. How do notes change as a guitar string is shortened?
2. Explain how to play a tune on a one-stringed instrument.
3. What is the difference between a loud note and a soft note? Draw a diagram showing loud waves and soft waves.

SOUND AND THICKNESS

Inside a grand piano. The thick strings, on the pianist's left, make low notes. These are also the longest strings. The strings decrease in length and thickness to produce the higher notes.

Look at the strings on a guitar, on a violin, or inside a piano. You will see that each string is a different thickness. Pluck the strings, or strike the keys. You will find that the thicker strings make lower notes than the thinner strings. The thicker strings are heavier and thus cannot vibrate as quickly as the thinner strings. As you know from page 18, slower vibrations give a lower note. If you look at stringed instruments (violin, viola, cello, and double bass), you will notice that not only are the lower-sounding instruments bigger, but that their strings are also thicker.

ACTIVITIES

MAKING TAPPING STICKS OR CLAVES

YOU NEED
• **2 thin, identical, bamboo garden stakes** • **2 thicker, identical garden stakes** • **a ruler** • **a clamp** • **a saw**

WARNING: be very careful when using a saw.

1 Look at the bamboo. You are going to cut identical pairs of sticks, which will make pairs of claves.

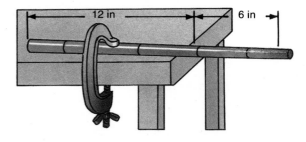

2 Take a thin bamboo cane. Set it in a clamp. Cut off a 6-inch length and a 12-inch length from the stake.

3 Now clamp the other thin piece.
4 Saw off identical claves: one 6-inch, the other 12 inches.
5 Repeat this with the thicker canes.

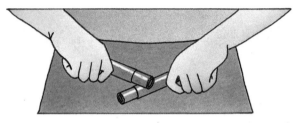

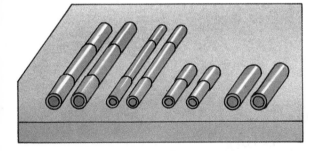

6 You should now have 4 pairs of matching claves—a thin 6-inch pair, a thin 12-inch pair, a thick 6-inch pair and a thick 12-inch pair.
7 Tap the thin 6-inch pair together. Listen to the sound.

8 Tap the thin 12-inch pair together. How is the sound different?
9 Tap the thick 6-inch pair together. Listen to the sound.
10 Tap the thick 12-inch pair together. How is this sound different?
11 Compare the sounds made from your thin 6-inch pair and your thick 6-inch pair. What do you hear?
12 What do you notice about thickness and the note produced?
13 Check your ideas by comparing the thin and thick 12-inch pairs.

SOUNDS FROM NAILS

YOU NEED

- **a hammer**
- **nails of different thicknesses, but the same length**
- **a thick block of wood**
- **a pencil**

1 Hammer the nails into the block of wood. Check that they do not touch each other.

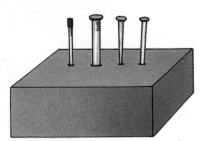

2 Make sure that each nail sticks out of the wood as far as the others.
3 Tap each nail in turn with a pencil.
4 Which nails make the highest notes? Which make the lowest notes?

WARNING: be very careful when hammering nails.

TEST YOURSELF

1. If a thin string and a thick string are the same length, which produces the higher note when plucked?
2. Draw sound waves that you might expect from a thick and a thin string of the same length.

SOUND AND TENSION

Look at a guitar. Each string is fixed to a block at one end and wound around a tuning peg at the other end. The peg can be turned to tighten or loosen the string—this is called tuning. If the string is wound more around the peg, the string is tightened and makes a higher note. If it is loosened, the note is lower. Tightening or loosening a string changes its tension.

A guitar's strings are made so that, when they are all at the correct tension, they play six notes—E, A, D, G, B, and another, higher E. A guitarist knows what these notes sound like when compared with each other, and tunes the strings by twisting the pegs until the notes sound

right. When this is done, the guitar has been tuned. Sometimes, the guitarist uses a special set of tuned pipes to hear the correct notes.

There are many stringed instruments. Each one needs to be tuned to its particular range of notes. Stringed instruments include the guitar, piano, violin, viola, cello, and double bass. There are also many other stringed instruments, which are all tuned with pegs.

Most notes on the piano have two or three strings wound around separate pegs. The piano tuner must tighten or loosen these pegs until the strings are perfectly in tune.

ACTIVITY

YOU NEED

- **a hammer**
- **a nail**
- **a length of wood (not balsa) about 15 inches long**
- **a guitar or violin string**
- **a large plastic bag**
- **some large stones**
- **2 pencils**
- **a ruler**

1 Hammer the nail in one end of the block of wood.
2 Tie one end of the string to the nail.
3 Fill a plastic bag with a few stones.

4 Tie the plastic bag to the other end of the string.
5 Hold the wood on the table so that it does not slip while allowing the string and bag to hang over the edge.

6 Put two pencils under the string to hold it away from the wood. Measure the distance between pencils.
7 Pluck the string between the pencils. Listen to the sound.

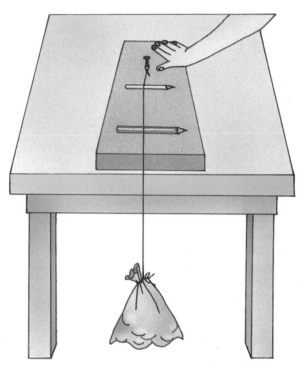

8 Put more stones in the bag. This will pull the string tighter. You have increased the string's tension.
9 Check that the pencils are the same distance apart.
10 Pluck the string again. How is the note different?
11 What do you notice about the string's tension and the note made?

TEST YOURSELF

1. How does the note produced by a vibrating string change when the tension is changed?
2. How do you change the tension of a string on a guitar?

SOUND AND VOLUME

Left The trombone player (center) produces different notes by varying the length of the brass tube. He does this by sliding part of the tube backward and forward.

Below The girl playing the recorder varies the length of the tube by putting her fingers over the airholes at the front.

You already know that a higher sound can be made in three ways: by using a shorter string, a thinner string, or a tighter string. However, not all musical instruments have strings. Many instruments are pipes that are blown into in various ways.

Pipes come in different lengths and diameters because the notes that can be played on the pipe depend on the volume of air inside it. The recorder family is a good example of varying sizes of pipes. The smallest recorder is the descant, then come the treble, the tenor, and finally the bass. As you might guess the descant plays the highest notes and the bass, the lowest.

When the recorder is blown into, a column of air inside the pipe vibrates. A long column allows a large amount of air which produces a low note.

The amount of air in the column can also be increased by making the column of air fatter. The bass recorder is not only longer, but also wider than the descant, treble, or tenor.

A recorder has holes along its pipe. If you put a finger over the top hole, you

make a longer air column. Thus the note is lower. Other pipe instruments (also called wind instruments) work in roughly the same way. The instruments differ in the way they make the air column longer or shorter to vary the notes.

ACTIVITIES

PLAYING A BOTTLE ORGAN

YOU NEED

- **a set of identical glass bottles**
- **water**

1 Blow across the top of a bottle until you find the right position to make a note.
2 Put some water in the bottle. Blow again. How has the note changed? Is there more or less air in the bottle than before?

3 Make a bottle organ by filling each bottle with a different amount of water. Try to make a musical scale by adjusting the water level in each bottle.

4 Arrange the bottles in the order of the notes. What do you notice about the water levels?

PLAYING A CARDBOARD TROMBONE

YOU NEED

- **a long cardboard tube from a roll of towels, wax paper, or foil**
- **a tall glass jar**
- **water**

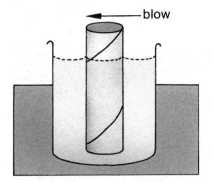

blow

1 Blow across the tube until you hear a note.

2 Fill the glass jar with water, almost to the top.

3 Put one end of the tube into the jar, so that it is just in the water.
4 Blow across the top of the tube. Listen to the note.
5 Slowly push the tube into the water as you blow. Listen to the note change.
6 Remember: as you push the tube into the water, the volume of air that is vibrating gets smaller as the water fills the tube.

TEST YOURSELF

1. What is the largest recorder called? Why is this a good name?
2. How does a note change as the volume of air changes?
3. How does a trombone produce different notes?

DRUMS

Drums are found in every human culture. They come in all shapes and sizes, and can be hit with parts of the hand, or special sticks. The drum's rhythm can be used for singing and dancing or to coordinate groups of people working together.

A drum usually consists of a skin (the drumhead) stretched tightly over a hollow frame. When the drummer hits the skin, it and the air inside the frame both vibrate. This causes the drum's sound to be made.

The note made by a drum depends on three things. The larger the drumhead, the lower the note is made, much like a longer or thicker guitar string. The tension in the drumhead is also important—the tighter the skin, the higher the note is made. The volume of air inside the frame also affects the sound—just as in a pipe, the larger the volume of air, the lower is the note. Therefore, a really low-noted drum is large, with a big, wide frame, and a slightly slack skin.

Some drums, such as large timpani (kettledrums) in orchestras, need to be tuned. As with a guitar, there are pegs for tightening or loosening. These pegs are found around the edge of the drumhead. Tightening the skin makes the note higher —loosening it makes the note lower.

Above There are two examples of drum-like instruments in this picture. The bass drum (center) plays a deep note, and the small tambourine is high-pitched.

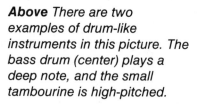

Left The drumhead of a drum in a steel band is divided into sections of differing size. Each section plays a different note when hit. The drums also vary in size.

ACTIVITIES

PLAYING A DRUM

YOU NEED

- **a small drum and a drumstick**
- **some rice grains**

1 Put some rice grains on the drumhead. Spread them around.

2 Gently tap the drumhead with the drumstick. What do you hear?

3 What happens to the rice? Why? Hit the drumhead a bit harder. What happens? Why?

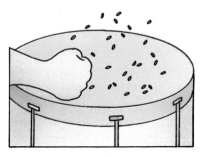

VOICE VIBRATIONS

YOU NEED

- **a plastic bottle or cardboard tube**
- **a balloon cut open**
- **rubber bands**

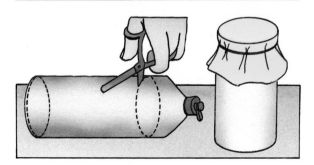

1 Cut off the ends of a plastic bottle to make a tube (or use a towel tube).

2 Stretch the balloon over one end of the tube.
3 Attach the balloon with several tightly-stretched rubber bands.
4 Speak into the other end of the tube.

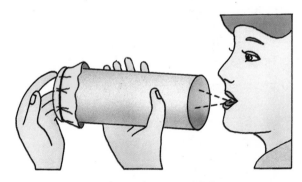

5 Lightly touch the balloon as you speak. What can you feel?
6 Speak louder into the tube and touch the balloon. What can you feel now?

TEST YOURSELF

1. Which makes a lower note, a small or a large drum?
2. How does a drum produce sound?
3. How would you tune a drum?

MUSIC AND NOISE

Look at a set of tuning forks. There are usually eight forks in a set, and each is a different size. The fork is "played" by striking it against a hard surface, which makes the prongs vibrate—much like plucking a string. The same rules also apply to tuning forks—the low notes are made by forks that are long and thick because they do not vibrate rapidly. A set of tuning forks make the notes C, D, E, F, G, A, B, C. The first and largest fork produces middle C. Then they go down in length and thickness, making the notes D to B. The smallest (eighth) fork is a C again, but this note is one octave higher than middle C. Tuning forks are very carefully made so that each one makes a pure sound with a regular wave having a fixed number of vibrations per second.

Noise occurs when a sound wave has no smooth pattern. It consists of a mixture of vibrations. The wave is all mixed up. For example, the hissing made by air escaping from a tire is not a pure sound. It is a noise. Its sound-wave pattern is irregular.

The sound from a tuning fork is pure and has a smooth, regular sound-wave pattern. The hammer's sound has an irregular, spiked wave, which is typical of a noise.

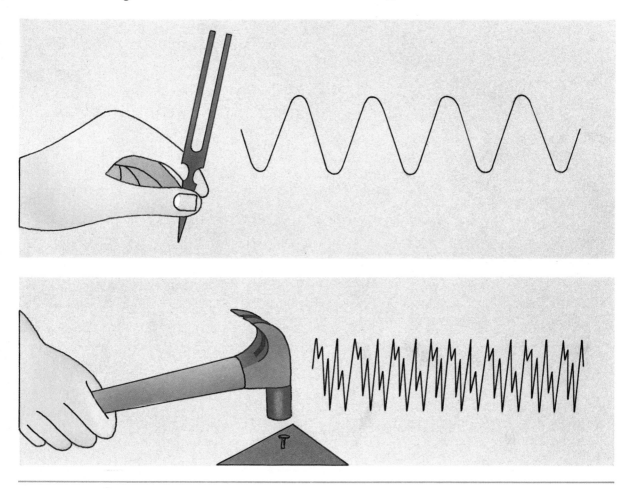

ACTIVITY

TUNING FORKS

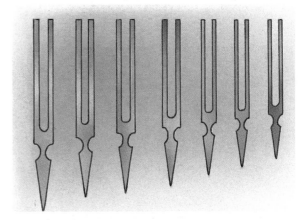

> YOU NEED
>
> - **a set of tuning forks**
> - **a large rubber eraser**
> - **a dish of water**
> - **a sheet of paper**

1 Choose 2 tuning forks. Compare their sizes. Which do you think will make the higher note?

2 Strike one tuning fork on the rubber eraser. Listen to the note it makes.

3 Strike the other tuning fork on the rubber eraser. Listen to this note. Which is higher? Were you right in your choice of the higher tuning fork?

4 Arrange the tuning forks in order of size. Strike each tuning fork in turn. What do you notice about the notes?

5 Strike a tuning fork on the rubber eraser. Hold it against the edge of a sheet of paper. What happens?

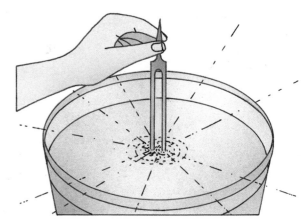

6 Touch some water with a vibrating tuning fork. What happens?

TEST YOURSELF

1. How does a tuning fork make its sound?
2. Which makes a higher note—a large or a small tuning fork?
3. What is the difference between a sound and a noise? Draw diagrams to help illustrate your answer.

HOW SOUND TRAVELS

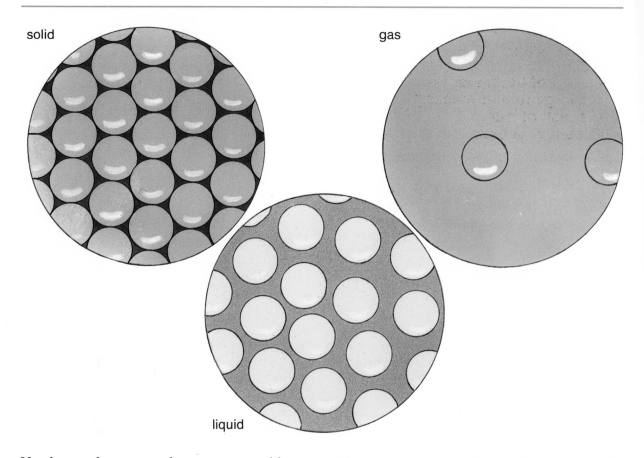

solid

gas

liquid

You know that a sound wave is started by something that is moving. The moving object pushes the particles of the substance around it. These particles then pass the energy on to the next particles, and so on, causing the energy of the movement to travel throughout the whole substance. This movement of particles is the sound wave.

Like anything that travels, sound has speed—how far it moves during a given time. The speed of a sound depends on the substance through which the sound is traveling.

Sound can travel through any substance—solid, liquid, or gas. Substances are made up of particles, which can be

It is easy to pass sound energy from one particle to another, if those particles are very close together.

moved as described above. In a gas, the particles are far apart. Much of the energy of the moving object is lost in pushing the gas particles large distances until they hit other particles. Thus the speed of sound through gas is slow.

The particles in a liquid and in a solid are much closer together. Thus not so much of the energy is lost in moving the particles until they hit other particles. This means that the speed of sound in liquids and in solids is much faster than it is in gases.

ACTIVITY

YOU NEED

- **a tuning fork**
- **a rubber eraser**
- **a ruler or measuring tape**

1 Ask a friend to strike the tuning fork on the rubber eraser and hold it in the air, 6 feet away from you.

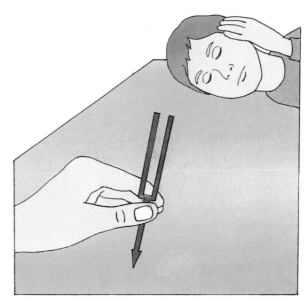

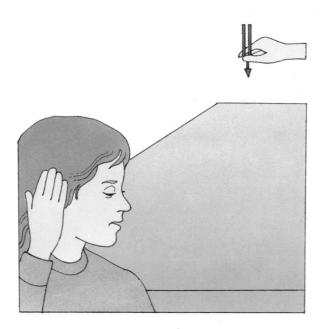

2 Put your hand over one ear and listen to the sound.

3 Now put your ear against a long table and cover the other ear as before.

4 Ask your friend to strike the tuning fork again, but this time to hold the base of it firmly against the table 6 feet away from your ear.

5 Which is louder—the sound in air or in wood?

6 Now try this experiment by ringing the tuning fork on the door, the wall, the floor, and a metal pipe.

7 Make sure that the fork is always 6 feet from your ear.

8 Which substance carries sound best? In other words, which makes the tuning fork sound loudest?

TEST YOURSELF

1. How are sound waves passed through a substance?
2. Why does a solid carry sound better than air?
3. Describe how you would test whether a metal ruler carries sound better than a wooden ruler.

YOUR EARS

The ear can be divided into three parts: the outer ear, the middle ear, and the inner ear. The outer ear, or auricle, is the part that you can see. Like a drum, the eardrum is a tightly stretched membrane. The auricle is shaped to channel sound into the middle ear.

The middle ear starts at the eardrum. It vibrates when you hear sounds. There must be air on both sides of the eardrum for it to vibrate. The air comes up from your throat through a narrow tube to your middle ear.

Three bones (the tiniest in your body) help the sound travel from the eardrum to the inner ear. They are the hammer, anvil, and stirrup. They are held tightly together by muscles, so there is no sound loss. The eardrum vibrates against the hammer, which passes the vibrations on to the anvil, and then to the stirrup. Bone is very dense, so sound moves quickly and efficiently.

The inner ear includes organs that help keep balance (the semicircular canals) and the hearing nerves. Some nerve cells are inside the cochlea, which is a coiled structure. The cochlea is full of liquid that surrounds the nerve cells.

Sound travels from the stirrup to the nerve cells. The stirrup vibrates against a small membrane called the oval window. This transmits the vibrations to the round window, below the oval window. The end of the cochlea touches the round window, so the vibrations are passed to the fluid in the cochlea, and then to the nerve cells. They send messages to the brain, which go to the sound memory for analysis.

This diagram shows the main features of the human ear.

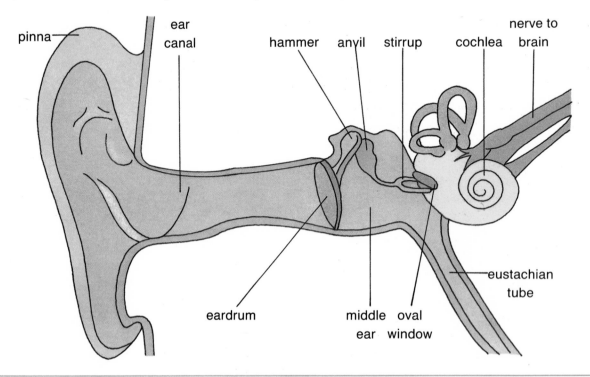

ACTIVITY

SOUND TRAVELS THROUGH BONE

<table>
<tr><td>

YOU NEED

- **a watch with a quiet tick**

</td></tr>
</table>

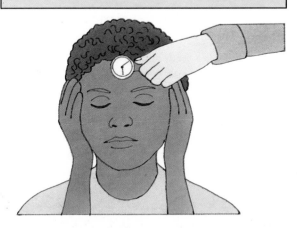

1 Put your hands over your ears. Ask a friend to hold the watch on your forehead. Can you hear the watch tick?
2 The sound is being carried to your ears through the bones of your skull.

3 Ask your friend to hold the watch to the top, back, and each side of your head. Listen to the sound. Does it change?

4 Ask your friend to hold the watch to your chin. Your chin is part of your jaw bone, which is held to your skull by muscles. Notice how much quieter the watch sounds.

Right A diagram of the three semicircular canals of the inner ear. The semicircular canals help you balance by sending information to your brain about your position in space. There is one canal for each direction of movement. Each canal is filled with a liquid which flows over special nerve cells in the canal when your body changes position.

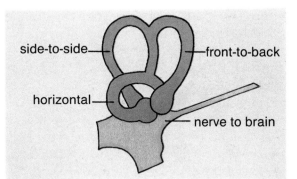

TEST YOURSELF

1. What are the three main parts of the ear called?
2. How does sound travel through the middle ear?
3. Where are your sound-sensitive nerve cells?

DEAFNESS

Left *A deaf theater play. These totally deaf people are using sign language to communicate to each other and to the audience.*

Below *This girl is partially deaf and wears a hearing aid.*

Deafness, which means a loss of hearing, can be partial or total. Deafness is caused by problems in the middle ear or inner ear. Middle-ear deafness means that sound is not being passed from the eardrum to the oval window. Inner-ear deafness can be a result of no sound-nerve messages being sent to the brain. There are many causes of both kinds of deafness.

Deafness can last for a short time (temporary) or for a lifetime (permanent). Most of us have felt the effects of temporary deafness and know how uncomfortable and inconvenient it is. It usually happens when the air pressure in the middle ear is different from the outside air pressure. This means that the eardrum cannot vibrate properly and pass on the sound waves. A head cold will often block the tube going from the throat to the ear. This alters the pressure in the middle ear causing temporary deafness. You can get a similar effect when flying. The air pressure in the cabin of an aircraft changes suddenly, especially on takeoff and landing.

If something is wrong with the hammer, anvil, or stirrup bones in the middle ear, sound vibrations will not be passed on properly. This causes partial, permanent deafness. The condition can be helped by a hearing aid or corrected by surgery.

The bones in the middle ear are held together by muscles, which can be damaged by loud noises. If you are in the presence of very loud noises, you will notice that you find it hard to hear afterward. But your hearing usually comes back after a while. This is a temporary, partial deafness. If you hear loud sounds for a long time—for example, at work, or often listening to very loud music—the deafness can be permanent.

Inner-ear deafness is more difficult to correct. It is usually caused by damaged sound nerves, resulting in no signals to the brain. In this case, the person is permanently, totally deaf and has difficulty speaking.

Most people have one ear that is stronger than the other. For about 60 percent of people, this is the left ear.

ACTIVITY

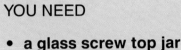

YOU NEED

- **a glass screw top jar containing dried peas**
- **a folded paper towel**

1 Ask a friend to sit on a chair and cover eyes with the towel.

2 Rattle the jar of peas. Try to make the rattle the same each time. When you rattle the peas, your friend has to point in the direction of the sound. Try rattling in front, behind, to the left, the right, high up and low down.

3 Check that you rattle at about the same distance each time.
4 Is there any direction from which your friend finds it difficult to detect sounds?

5 Repeat the experiment, but ask your partner to cover one ear. Your friend can only hear with the one ear, and is "temporarily deaf" in the other.
6 How does this affect the result?
7 Repeat the experiment using only the other ear. Is one ear stronger than the other?

TEST YOURSELF

1. What could cause the eardrum temporarily not to vibrate properly?
2. What damage could be caused by subjecting your ears to loud sounds?
3. Which kind of permanent deafness is most difficult to correct?

MAKING SOUNDS LOUDER

Left *This hare has enormous external ears that catch sounds and channel them into its middle ear. This is quite common among animals that are hunted by others.*

Below *This chart shows the loudness of some familiar sounds.*

You have already found out how sounds are made, how they travel and how they are received. Once a sound has been created, it can move out from its source in all directions, much like ripples moving outward from a stone that has hit water. Standing in one place, you can hear only part of the sound; the rest is going everywhere else. However, if the sound is somehow beamed directly at you, then you hear the whole sound. This makes it much louder, as all the sound energy is reaching you. People sometimes cup their hands behind their ears to hear better. They are making a "funnel" to catch more of the

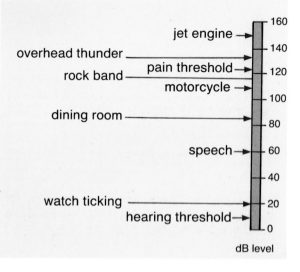

jet engine → 160
overhead thunder — 140
rock band — pain threshold → 120
motorcycle → 100
dining room — 80
speech → 60
40
watch ticking — 20
hearing threshold → 0

dB level

sound energy, like an old-fashioned ear trumpet. We can also use megaphones to direct sound to other people when we speak. They work in just the same way.

The loudness of a sound depends on how high its wave is (its amplitude). The higher the wave, the louder is the sound, because the sound wave has more energy.

If you are playing a guitar and want to make a louder sound, you pluck the strings harder. Thus you use more energy.

The loudness of a sound is measured in decibels (dB). Very loud noises are over 120 dB. A jet engine is about 150 dB and one of the quietest sounds is the rustling of dry leaves, which is about 10 dB.

ACTIVITY

MEGAPHONES AND TRUMPETS

YOU NEED

- **2 large sheets of stiff paper**
- **cellophane tape**
- **scissors**

WARNING: be careful not to make loud sounds during this activity.

1 Twist one sheet of paper around to make a cone.
2 Check that it is open at both ends.

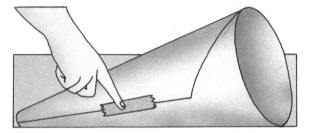

3 Hold the cone together with tape.

4 Make a second cone.
5 Ask a friend to talk to you. Move away until you can just hear.

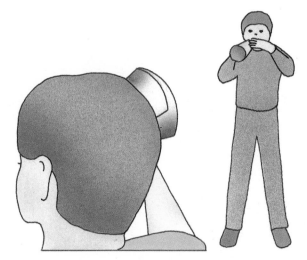

6 Now ask your friend to use one cone as a megaphone and talk into it in the same tone. Make sure it is pointing toward you. Does the sound seem louder? Hold the other cone as an ear trumpet. Point it toward the megaphone. Is the sound louder?

TEST YOURSELF

1. Why do megaphones make a sound louder?
2. Draw a sound wave of a loud sound and of a quiet sound.
3. What is the amplitude of a wave?

MUFFLING SOUNDS

Many sounds in our environment are un-wanted noises. To scientists, noise is caused by irregular sound waves (see page 28). We call noise any sound that is unpleasant, not wanted, or too loud.

Each person has a different idea of noise. For example, you may be playing a record in your room. You enjoy listening to the music, but the sound could be carried through the walls of your room to some-one who does not like your record. To that person, your record is noise. Some noises are not just annoying. They may also be dangerous because they are so loud. There-fore it is important to control noise. There are many ways of doing this.

This helicopter pilot is on the helipad of an oil rig. Because it is very noisy, he is wearing ear protectors to protect his hearing.

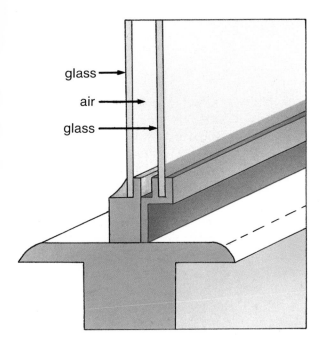

glass →

air →

glass →

You know that solid objects carry sound waves well but gases, such as air, do not. If there is an air gap between the walls of two rooms, sound is not carried well through the walls. The wall is insulated by the air.

Because they are full of airholes, springy objects do not carry sound as well as rigid objects. Sound-proofing, or acoustic tiles are springy. They absorb sound and transmit little. Thick carpets insulate a room in the same way. If a noise level is dangerous, such as in some types of work, ear protectors can be worn to reduce the noise to a safe level.

Left *A diagram of double glazing, or double panes of glass. The air between the panes of glass acts as a sound insulator.*

ACTIVITY

SOUND-PROOFING A FLOOR

YOU NEED

- **an alarm clock**
- **sound-insulating materials to test, such as newspaper, different fabrics, styrofoam packing material**

1 Put the ringing alarm clock on a table. Listen to the sound.

2 Put material under the ringing clock. Is the ringing sound quieter or louder?

3 Put another material underneath the clock, in place of the first. What happens now?

4 Test all your materials. Which is the best insulator?

TEST YOURSELF

1. What are the two definitions of noise?
2. How do acoustic tiles work?
3. What is one reason to use double glazing?

ECHOES

Have you ever shouted in a tunnel and heard your voice bounce back as an echo? Your voice was reflected back to you from the tunnel walls. An echo is a reflected sound. Echoes usually occur when sound waves in air meet a solid, such as a wall. They can also be caused when sound hits a solid after traveling through a liquid.

Echoes can be useful or annoying. In a concert hall, echoes ruin a performance. If the walls and ceiling are too hard or too flat they make good reflecting surfaces for the sound waves—just as a highly-polished mirror gives the clearest reflection of yourself.

Echoes can be used to give vital information. Because sound waves reflect at the boundary between two different substances, such as between liquid and solid, equipment such as sonar and ultrasound can be used. One type of sonar device sends out high-frequency sound waves from a ship to the sea bed to keep the vessel in safe waters. An ultrasound scanner, used for giving images of babies before they are born, works in roughly the same way.

Bats use echoes to navigate as they fly during the night. Again, this system works on the same principle as sonar and ultrasound. The bat sends out high-pitched squeaks, which bounce off objects in the bat's flight path. The echoes reach the bat, allowing it to adjust its course to avoid the obstacles. Many bats have very large ears which catch as much of the reflected sound as possible.

Ultrasonic waves are bounced off the baby in the womb. A computer interprets the echoes to give a picture of the baby.

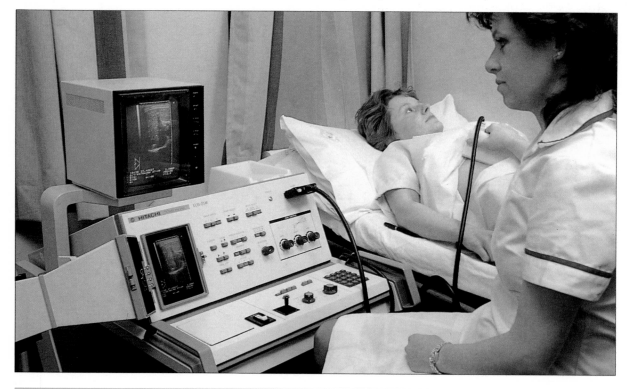

At night, bats use echolocation to guide them in flight. They send out clicking sounds, which bounce off objects and return to the bat. The echoes build up a "sound" picture of the surroundings.

BOUNCING SOUNDS AROUND CORNERS

YOU NEED

- **2 paper cones**
- **a metal tray**

1 Open a room's door. Sit outside with the wall between you and a friend.

2 Ask your friend to hold a cone to her ear as an ear trumpet.

3 Hold your cone as a megaphone. Point it to the tray, outside the door.

4 Talk quietly into the megaphone. Can your friend hear what you are saying? Alter the angle and position of the tray until the sound is loudest.

5 Note the angle at which the sound is bounced. Trace the sound's path.

TEST YOURSELF

1. What is an echo?
2. How does sonar work?
3. Which reflects sound better—styrofoam tiles or a brick wall?

THE SPEED OF SOUND

You already know how sound travels and that the speed of sound depends on the substance through which it travels. We are most used to the speed of sound in air, which is about 1,000 feet per second. This means that someone 1,000 feet away from you will hear your handclap one second after you clap. It is about 750 miles per hour, which in aircraft is called Mach 1. Twice the speed of sound is called Mach 2, and so on. If an aircraft travels faster than the speed of sound, it is flying at supersonic speed. This can create a shock wave, called the sonic boom, behind the aircraft. Sonic booms can break windows.

An interesting effect was discovered by the Austrian scientist, C.J. Doppler, in 1842. You have probably noticed this effect. Think about the sound of a siren on a police car as the car speeds toward you and then travels past. The sound of the siren changes from high-pitched to low pitched. Why? When the car speeds toward you, the sound waves are pushed closer together. Closer sound waves means the wavelength is in turn shorter, making the

Above *Concorde, the commercial supersonic aircraft.*

Below *The Doppler Effect. As the sound source moves closer, the waves are pushed together. Thus the listener hears a higher sound. The opposite happens when the sound source is moving away.*

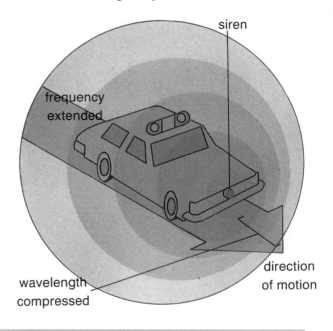

siren

frequency extended

wavelength compressed

direction of motion

sound higher pitched than if the siren were standing still.

When the car speeds away the waves are spread apart. Now the wavelength is longer, giving a lower note. This effect is called the Doppler Effect.

THUNDER AND LIGHTNING

Lightning is a big electrical spark that travels at high speed from clouds to the ground. Thunder is a sonic boom made when lightning passes through air. You can use your knowledge of the speed of sound to find out how far you are away from lightning.

You can see lightning as soon as it occurs because the speed of light is so fast. Look for the flash, then count the time in seconds until you hear the thunder. Sound takes about 5 seconds to travel 1 mile. So thunder 10 seconds after the flash would mean that the storm is 2 miles away. This is interesting to do, as you will notice that the storm moves around until it is over or too far away to be heard. However, make sure that you are indoors when you do this. Lightning is very dangerous especially when you are outdoors or under a tree.

Forked lightning over a city at night. This kind of lightning can be very dangerous.

RECORDING SOUND

Thomas Edison made the first, scratchy, sound recording on a cylindrical phonograph record in 1877. Since then, sound reproduction methods have been improved so much that the most modern equipment might make you think that you have your favorite band or singer in the room with you.

Sound reproduction is based on the fact that sound is a form of energy, and that one form of energy can be changed into another. In all recording techniques, there are two vital parts: the microphone and the loudspeaker. The microphone usually has a moving part, much like an eardrum, which picks up sound waves and vibrates. Inside the microphone, sound energy is turned into electrical energy, which can then be sent through an electrical current.

The loudspeaker is the opposite of the microphone. It turns the electrical energy back into sound energy. A moving part turns the electrical messages into sound vibrations. Sound waves are then sent out to the listener.

Some energy is lost when sound energy is changed into electrical energy and back again. A device called an amplifier is used to build up the electrical energy so that sound coming out of the loudspeaker is louder. The level of sound can then be adjusted using the volume control.

Thomas Edison listening to one of his recordings on his phonograph. Recordings were made by scratching grooves onto a metal cylinder, then played back by running a needle through those grooves.

Left *This girl can listen to her favorite music on her personal stereo, without disturbing anyone else.*

Below *Compact discs are gradually replacing records. They are "read" by a laser beam instead of a stylus, so they last almost indefinitely.*

Between the microphone and the loud-speaker, there must be a means of storing the electrical waves from the microphone. There is a whole range of modern technology that can be used for this job. The waves can be stored on records, cassette tape, compact discs. On discs lasers are used to make the disc's surface. A laser beam "reads" the marks and turns the messages that it has read back into electrical waves or pulses. Before going to the loudspeaker, they pass through the amplifier. This makes the sound louder. The pulses then go to the loudspeaker to be turned into sound waves that can then be heard by the human ear.

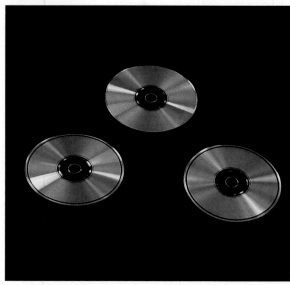

Glossary

Anvil   A tiny bone in the middle ear. It conducts sound waves to the inner ear.

Auricle   The outer ear.

Cartilage   A firm, elastic substance that forms part of bone structure.

Claves   Sticks, made of hard wood, that are struck together to make a hollow sound.

Cochlea   A part of the inner ear which converts sound vibrations to nerve signals.

Decibel   A measurement of sound intensity.

Eardrum   A vibrating skin that separates the outer ear from the middle ear. It passes sound vibrations to the bones of the middle ear.

Echo   The reflection of a sound wave.

Frequency   The rate at which something happens, for example, the number of sound vibrations per second.

Glockenspiel   A musical instrument that is made of a row of metal bars of different lengths. These are hit with a pair of small hammers to produce notes of different pitch.

Hammer   A tiny bone in the middle ear. It conducts sound vibrations from the eardrum.

Larynx   The box-like space at the top of the windpipe. It contains the vocal cords.

Lightning   A spark or flash in the sky, caused by a sudden electrical discharge from a cloud.

Loudspeaker   An instrument that converts electrical energy to sound.

Mach 1   The speed of sound. Mach numbers are named after Ernst Mach, who devised the system of speed measurement. Mach 2 is twice the speed of sound, Mach 3 is three times, and so on.

Megaphone   A funnel-shaped device for increasing or directing sound.

Membrane   A thin sheet or film.

Microphone   An instrument that converts sound waves into electrical energy.

Noise   Sound produced by irregular vibrations. The sound waves have no smooth pattern. Also any sound that is unpleasant, unwanted, or too loud.

Octave   The eight-note distance between two musical notes of the same name, such as C.

Pinna   Part of the external, or outer, ear. A fleshy flap that collects sound and channels it into the ear.

Pitch   The highness or lowness of a musical note. Notes of different pitch have different frequencies.

Reflection   In science, a wave that is bounced off an object. In sound, an echo from bounced sound waves.

Semicircular canals   Found in the inner ear, three canals that tell the brain about position in space; they help with balance.

Sonic boom   A loud bang from the shock wave created by an object traveling faster than the speed of sound.

Stethoscope   An instrument used by doctors to listen to the sounds made by the heart and lungs.

Stirrup   A tiny bone in the middle ear that helps conduct sound vibrations to the inner ear.

Stylus   A needle attached to the cartridge in the arm of a record player. It travels in the grooves and transmits the vibrations to a sensing device in the cartridge.

Supersonic Faster than the speed of sound.

Tension The tight stretching of something, such as a string.

Thunder The sound made from the shock wave caused by lightning passing through air.

Transparent An object that lets all visible light through it.

Tuning fork A metal instrument that is made to vibrate at only one frequency. It can be used when tuning instruments.

Vibrations Movements backward and forward or up and down.

Wavelength One full wave movement, such as from the crest of one wave to the crest of the next.

Books to Read

The Magic of Sound, Larry Kettelkamp (Morrow, 1982)

Music & Sound, Mark Pettigrew (Franklin Watts, 1987)

Light & Sound, Peter Riley (David & Charles, 1987)

Sound & Recording, Keith Wicks (Franklin Watts, 1982)

Picture Acknowledgments

The author and publishers would like to thank the following for allowing illustrations to be reproduced in this book: Chapel Studios, *cover*, 38; Bruce Coleman Ltd, 12; Sally and Richard Greenhill, 34 (below); National Film Archive, 8 (right); Science Photo Library, 15, 42; Sefton Photo Library, 26; Topham Picture Library, *cover*, frontispiece, 22, 24, 34, (above), 44; Tim Woodcock, 45 (above); ZEFA, 6, 7, 8 (left), 18, 20, 36, 40, 43, 45 (below). All artwork is by Marilyn Clay and Peter Bull. Cover artwork by Jenny Hughes.

Index